The Bible Discovery Collection

Bible Animals

GOD'S WORLD BOOK CLUB
EDITION

P.O. Box 2330 • Asheville, NC 28802 • 1-800-951-2665

Fly

Editorial Director LaVonne Neff
Editor Karen Ball
Creative Director William Paetzold
Designer Raelee Lehman
Design Research & Acquisitions Marlene S. Muddell
Typesetting Gwen Elliott
Development Team Bruce B. Barton, D.Min.;
James C. Galvin, Ed. D.,; Michael Kendrick; Daryl J. Lucas;
David R. Veerman, M.Div.; Neil S. Wilson, M.Div.
Reviewers C. Donald Cole, radio pastor, Moody Bible Institute;
Albert J. Smith, Ph. D., professor of biology, Wheaton College;
Dr. Kenneth N. Taylor, chairman of the board, Tyndale House Publishers;
James D. Worthington, Ph. D., dean of the School of Education,
Seattle Pacific University

Illustrations: Page 38 copyright © 1989 by Robert Florczak;
Page 51 copyright © 1989 by Don Gabriel;
Pages 15 top, 57 copyright © 1989 by Blas Gallego;
Page 42 center copyright © 1989 by Sergio Martinez;
Pages 34 center, 35 center, 44, 45 copyright © 1989 by Joseph Miralles;
Page 50 copyright © 1989 by Joan Pelaez;
Cover and pages 1-63 copyright © 1991 by Paul Turnbaugh.

All other illustrations copyright © 1989
by Tyndale House Publishers, Inc. All rights reserved.
Pages 17 bottom, 30 top, 39 by Donald Kueker; Pages 7 top, 51 top by Jeffrey Terreson.

Photos: Pages 20, 21, 25 top by Nancy Adams;
Pages 22 top, 25 center, 29 bottom, 31 by Anthony Bannister/ABPL;
Pages 28, 35 by Anthony Bannister/NHPA; Page 38 top by John Brooks;
Page 41 center by Daphne Carew/ABPL; Pages 9 bottom, 16 top left, 23, 48 bottom, 57
by Ed Degginger; Page 52 by Phil Degginger; Page 46 by Nigel Dennis/ABPL;
Page 47 top by Nigel Dennis/NHPA; Page 27 top left by Jeanne Drake;
Page 5 top by Robert Fine; Page 61 top by Doris Friedman; Page 11 by Milton J. Griffith;
Pages 4 bottom, 17 top by Betty Groskin; Pages 14, 41 top by Clem Haagner/ABPL;
Page 5 bottom by Thomas Henion; Pages 49, 56 center, 61 bottom by Breck Kent;
Pages 4, 55, 58 by Stephen Kirkpatrick; Page 16 top right by Tim Liversedse/ABPL;
Page 36 by Dr. Alan K. Mallams; Pages 3 center, 10 top, 25 bottom, 26 top,
29 center, 37, 42 top, 43, 48 center by Zev Radovan, Israel;
Page 22 center by Howard Robson, Tulsa; Page 3 bottom by Samuel Saylor;
Page 10 center by John Shaw/NHPA; Pages 8 top, 47 center, 54 bottom by Lynn Stone;
Page 53 by Bob Taylor; Page 24 by Dave Welling.

Published by Tyndale House Publishers, Inc.
351 Executive Drive P.O. Box 80 Wheaton, Illinois 60189-0080

Scripture verses are taken from *The Living Bible* © 1971
owned by assignment by KNT Charitable Trust. All rights reserved.

© 1992 by Tyndale House Publishers, Inc
All rights reserved
Printed In the United States of America

99 98 97 96 95
8   7   6   5   4

Goldfish

Lion

Frog

Bronze snake

The Bible Discovery Collection

Bible Animals

Panther

Written by
BRUCE B. BARTON, D.Min.
JAMES C. GALVIN, Ed.D.
J. MICHAEL KENDRICK
DARYL J. LUCAS
DAVID R. VEERMAN, M.Div.
NEIL S. WILSON, M.Div.

Ibis

Tyndale House Publishers, Inc.
Wheaton, Illinois

Contents

Great
Blue Heron

Harlequin
Cabbage bug

Beluga
Whale

Tree
Frog

"All the animals of field and forest are mine! The cattle on a thousand hills! And all the birds upon the mountains!"
Psalm 50:10-11

Zebra

Starfish

Black Leopard

CONCORDIA UNIVERSITY LIBRARY
PORTLAND, OR 97211

First Animals

God created the world and everything in it with a word. Ever since, people have been studying his wonderful creation. Adam named the animals (Genesis 2:19-20). Solomon studied animals, birds, snakes, and fish (1 Kings 4:33). And new kinds of animals are still being discovered. Scientists have identified more than one million species so far, and they are identifying more every year. "O Lord, what a variety you have made! And in wisdom you have made them all! The earth is full of your riches" (Psalm 104:24).

The Bible mentions many animals. Some helped people and some hurt people. In this book you will meet many of these animals and learn many fascinating things about them. Knowing more about Bible animals will help you better understand the Bible.

Sea and Sky Animals

The very first animals God created were those that live in the seas and skies. These two groups of animals include one of the smallest animals (the hummingbird) and one of the largest animals (the whale). "Then God said, 'Let the waters teem with fish and other life, and let the skies be filled with birds of every kind.' So God created great sea animals, and every sort of fish and every kind of bird. And God looked at them with pleasure, and blessed them all. 'Multiply and stock the oceans,' he told them, and to the birds he said, 'Let your numbers increase. Fill the earth!' That ended the fifth day" (Genesis 1:20-23).

Land Animals

After filling the seas and skies with fish and birds, God created animals to live on the land. "And God said, 'Let the earth bring forth every kind of animal—cattle and reptiles and wildlife of every kind.' And so it was. God made all sorts of wild animals and cattle and reptiles. And God was pleased with what he had done." (Genesis 1:24-25).

God made hundreds of thousands of kinds of animals. Can you identify the animals on the cover?

Front cover: (clockwise from the top) Lobster, bush baby, goldfish, lion, dolphin, frog, chick, elephant, hummingbird, hornet, fieldmouse, swallowtail butterfly. Back cover: (clockwise from the top) Cat eyes, blue cheek butterfly fish, rabbits, heron, Red Sea grouper, mandrill, walrus, bald eagle.

Man and Woman

God's final creation was the most wonderful of all: man and woman! He made a man from "the dust of the ground," and he made a woman from the man's ribs. Then he gave them the whole world for their home. "And God blessed them [the first man and woman] and told them, 'Multiply and fill the earth and subdue it; you are masters of the fish and birds and all the animals. And look! I have given you the seed-bearing plants throughout the earth, and all the fruit trees for your food. And I've given all the grass and plants to the animals and birds for their food.' Then God looked over all that he had made, and it was excellent in every way. This ended the sixth day" (Genesis 1:28-31).

SEVEN DAYS OF CREATION

First Day	Light
Second Day	Sky and water
Third Day	Sea and earth
Fourth Day	Sun, moon, and stars
Fifth Day	Fish and birds
Sixth Day	Land animals, man and woman
Seventh Day	Rest and enjoyment

Homes & Habitats

Bible animals had homes in many different kinds of places. Some lived in between rocks or in the desert sand. Others lived in tall grasses or even right among their human neighbors. Still others lived in wetlands or under the water. Altogether, animals of the Bible lands had at least five different kinds of homes and habitats: desert, hill, valley, plateau, and plain.

Green Tree Frog

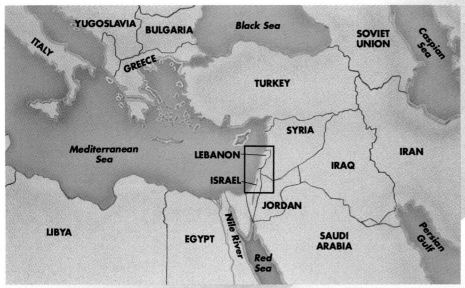

The Bible Lands
What we call "Bible lands" is a small area at the east end of the Mediterranean Sea. The Mediterranean Sea falls in between the continents of Africa (to the south), Europe (to the north), and Asia (to the east). This map shows the countries that surround the Mediterranean today.

Animals That Lived on the Plain
The coastal plain is the lowland near the Mediterranean Sea. In Bible times it was the main route used by caravans traveling between Egypt and Damascus. These caravans almost always included pack animals such as *camels* and *donkeys*, and *war horses* in times of war. Animals that lived on the coastal plain included *birds, deer, frogs, wild boars, hare, mice, rats,* and *dogs.* These animals ate grasses, shrubs, insects, and other wildlife.

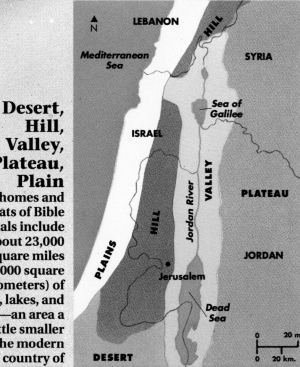

Lizard

Desert, Hill, Valley, Plateau, Plain
The homes and habitats of Bible animals include about 23,000 square miles (60,000 square kilometers) of land, lakes, and rivers—an area a little smaller than the modern country of Ireland.

Animals That Lived in the Desert
The land to the south and east of Israel is mostly rolling hills of dry, rocky soil. During the summer it is hot, with temperatures usually over 100° Fahrenheit (38° centigrade). These areas get less than eight inches (20.5 centimeters) of rain per year—only slightly more than Death Valley in the southwestern United States. Animals that lived in the desert regions in Bible lands included *lizards, geckos, land monitors, scorpions, gazelles, snakes, ants,* and *spiders.* Gazelles ate the sparse vegetation. Lizards, geckos, scorpions, and spiders ate insects. Snakes ate rodents. Land monitors ate whatever meat they could find.

Animals That Lived in the Hill Country

The hill country extends over 150 miles (250 kilometers) from Sinai in the south to Galilee in the north. The hills often have fertile land basins between them. Some of the hills in the north are almost 3,000 feet (900 meters) high. Animals that lived in the hill country included *bears, deer, gazelles, rock badgers, hyenas, wolves,* and *lions*. The Israelites used the hill country for grazing their *cattle, sheep,* and *goats*. Animals that had to run and hide from enemies found plenty of protection among the rocks and crags. Israelite shepherds had to guard their flocks from lions, wolves, and hyenas in the hills, just as they did on the plateau.

Wolf

Jordan River

Dead Sea

Animals That Lived in the Valley

There are many small valleys in Bible lands. The largest is the Rift Valley, which includes the Sea of Galilee, the Jordan River, and the Dead Sea. Animals that lived in valleys included *lions, bears, wild boars, frogs, mosquitoes, tortoises, birds,* and fish such as *carp, St. Peter's fish,* and *perch*. Vegetable-eating land animals ate the shrubs and grasses that grew near the water. Meat-eating animals ate the smaller animals that lived there. Because of the fresh water, valleys were always rich in vegetation and wildlife. Many animals used the thick grasses and trees as hiding places or dens.

Sea of Galilee

Tortoise

Fallow Deer

Animals That Lived on the Plateau

The land to the east of the Jordan River is called the Transjordan. It is the western part of the country of Jordan. This open, rolling land gets plenty of rain, making it very fertile. The Israelite tribes of Reuben and Gad settled there because it was perfect for grazing their livestock. (Numbers 32 and Joshua 1 in the Bible tell the story of how they chose this land.) Wild animals that lived on plateaus included *lions, leopards, gazelles,* and *deer*. The lions and leopards hunted and ate the gazelles and deer. They also hunted *cattle, goats,* and *sheep* owned by farmers.

Cattle & Goats

Few animals provided more useful service to the people of Israel than cattle and goats. They gave meat, milk, and cheese. They provided labor for plowing. Their hides were used as leather for clothing. They even gave the Israelites something to use as a sacrifice for sins.

In Bible times, goats and sheep often grazed together. Goats came in many colors—white, gray, brown, black, even spotted. Sometimes white goats mixed in with the herds of sheep, and it was hard to tell them apart. A shepherd who knew his animals by sight would have to separate them. Jesus spoke of separating the sheep from the goats to explain how he will one day separate those who love and obey him from those who don't (Matthew 25:31-33).

Ibex in the Negev

Nubian Ibex

Get Lost

Though goats were useful, they tended to wander off. Sheep, not being too bright, would sometimes follow the goats away from the shepherd—and end up lost. That is why the Bible calls evil people goats.

Goats

The Israelites depended on goats in many ways.

- One nanny goat can make up to six pints (2.8 liters) of milk a day.
- Goatskins could be used for leather and for bottles.
- Goat horns could be made into musical instruments.
- Some kinds of goat hair could be woven into rough cloth for stuffing pillows and making clothes. Since goathair clothing was rough and scratchy, usually poor people wore it. Some of God's people had only goatskins to wear (Hebrews 11:37).

Oxen: Bible-Time Tractors

The Hebrews used oxen to do many things. An ox could:

- pull a plow
- drag a threshing sledge (a flat board with teeth that separated grain from stalks)
- drive a water wheel
- pull a cart

For a farmer to lose his ox would be like a farmer today losing an expensive tractor. A person without an ox could not expect to make a good living, so people took very good care of these animals (Luke 13:15).

Masai Cattle

Cattle Facts

Cattle are mentioned about 450 times in the Bible. Domestic cattle were descendants of the wild ox (also called the auroch). Cattle were raised mostly for labor, food, and sacrifice. Because Israel did not have much grazing land, cattle could not be kept in large numbers. The hilly country of Upper Galilee was the best land for raising cattle (Psalm 50:10).

Animal Sacrifices

Bulls (male cattle) often were sacrificed as burnt offerings, fellowship offerings, or sin offerings. Both cows (female cattle) and goats were used as sacrifices for sins. Any animal that was sacrificed had to be completely free of defects (Leviticus 4:23). God accepted the animal's death as a substitute for the death of the person who had sinned (Leviticus 1:4).

What was an important restriction on the way goat meat could be cooked?

The Israelites were not allowed to boil a young goat (kid) in its mother's milk (Deuteronomy 14:21). This was because some of Israel's neighbors, the Canaanites, boiled young goats alive as a part of their violent and cruel fertility sacrifices. God wanted Israel's sacrifices to be humane.

Food Laws

Until we are old enough to cook for ourselves, others make sure that the food we eat is good for us. Because God cared about what his people ate, he gave them rules about what to eat and how to eat it. God gave these rules to show that Israel was to be different from the surrounding nations. He also wanted to protect his people from disease and health problems. Most of the eating rules that God gave Israel are in the book of Leviticus (chapters 11:1-47; 19:26; and 22:30). The rules may look strange to us today, but they made good sense. In those days there were no scientists or doctors to explain why something might be harmful or poisonous. And there were no refrigerators or chemicals to preserve food or to keep it from growing dangerous bacteria. God's rules about eating helped the Israelites avoid food that could make them sick—or even kill them!

Bible Menus

In Bible times, a typical meal might have included
- homemade barley bread
- milk or cheese
- grapes, figs, or dates
- fish
- pickled olives
- lentil soup

Rich people also ate
- nuts
- honey
- lamb, beef, or chicken

Lamb Stew

Clean or Unclean

The laws God gave Israel divided animals into two groups: animals allowed for eating and animals not allowed for eating. The animals that could be eaten were called "clean." The animals that could not be eaten were called "unclean." People could be "unclean," too. If someone touched any kind of dead animal, he was considered unclean. He could not take part in religious ceremonies (see Leviticus 11:39).

In fact, he had to stay away from everyone else until evening (see Leviticus 11:24-25).

Clean

OK to Eat

The Israelites were allowed to eat animals that chewed the cud and had hooves that were divided into two parts (Leviticus 11:1). Animals that chew the cud are called "ruminants." They chew and swallow the same food several times. This way they get the most out of the shrubs and grasses they eat. Ruminants with cloven hooves that were commonly eaten by God's people included goats, sheep, and cattle. Pigs have cloven hooves, but they do not chew the cud. Therefore, they were not to be eaten.

Fish

Fish were on God's "OK to Eat" list, and many Hebrews ate fish (Leviticus 11:9). Fishermen used dragnets to catch fish in the Sea of Galilee and the Mediterranean Sea. Jesus' disciples James and John fished on the Sea of Galilee. (See Mark 1:19.)

Unclean

Don't Touch!

- Scavengers such as the pig and rock badger were not to be eaten (Leviticus 11:4-7). There were good reasons for this. These animals often ate dead animals and carried disease and parasites such as tapeworms. If people ate these animals, they could become very sick and even die.

- Sea animals without fins and scales were forbidden (Leviticus 11:9-12). These included water snakes, lizards, eels, oysters, crabs, and lobsters. Some of them were poisonous, while others would spoil quickly and spread disease.

- Birds that ate other animals, especially dead animals, were forbidden as food (Leviticus 11:13-19). These birds included eagles, seagulls, ostriches, vultures, pelicans, and storks.

The dietary laws of the Old Testament do not apply to Christians today. God chose the apostle Peter to reveal this change. (See Acts 10:9-23 for the story of how this happened.) The apostle Paul also made it clear that the Jewish food laws no longer apply to believers in Christ (Romans 14:14).

The Israelites were allowed to eat one kind of insect. What was it?

They could eat jumping insects, such as grasshoppers (locusts) and crickets (Leviticus 11:21-22).

Birds

The Bible speaks of many birds, from the giant ostrich to the powerful eagle to the tiny sparrow. Birds were offered as sacrifices in the temple. They were eaten for dinner. They were used to decorate palaces. They carried messages. Birds were also used as symbols of God's Spirit, his might, and his care. In one of John's visions described in the book of Revelation, birds eat people! (Revelation 19:21).

Green Pigeons

Quail

Quail are one of the smallest game birds. They appear in the Bible only twice. On the first occasion, God caused a strong wind to carry a large flock of quail to the Israelites in the wilderness. This provided the hungry people with a much-needed meal (Exodus 16:1-13). The second time, God gave the same people quail again, in response to their complaining (Numbers 11:4-20, 31-34). But because the people had complained, many of them died in a plague soon after.

Pigeons and Doves

Pigeons and doves are mentioned in the Bible more often than any other bird. The Hebrews ate them and used them in sacrifices. They are very gentle birds, even when threatened. Jesus wanted his disciples to learn to be "harmless as doves" (Matthew 10:16).

Strange and Exotic Birds

Here are some of the more unusual birds mentioned in the Bible:

- *Cormorants*—Large seabirds that eat fish
- *Hoopoes*—Birds with long, curved bills
- *Black and Red Kites*—Hawk-like birds with long tails
- *Peacocks*—Birds with colorful, fan-shaped tails
  - *Vultures*—Birds that eat dead animals
    - *Bats*—Rodents, but listed with birds because they fly!

Chickens

Jesus said his love is like the love of a mother hen who "gathers her chicks under her wings" (Matthew 23:37). Peter was made to realize a mistake when a rooster crowed (Matthew 26:69-75).

Ostriches

Ostriches are the largest birds alive. They can grow as tall as eight feet (2.4 meters) and weigh as much as 300 pounds (136 kilograms). They can even outrun horses. Ostrich eggs are six to eight inches (15 to 20 centimeters) long and weigh up to three pounds (1.4 kilograms). Ostriches used to live in large numbers in the Middle East, but excessive hunting destroyed most of them. In the Bible, ostriches are noted for their strange habits (Job 39:13-18).

The Dove and the Olive Branch

When Noah received an olive branch from a dove, he knew that the Flood would soon be over (Genesis 8:10-11). Today the picture of a dove holding an olive branch is used by many as a symbol of peace. A dove is also a symbol of forgiveness, love, the Holy Spirit, and the church (John 1:32).

Sparrows

Sparrows were common in Bible times just as they are today. They were often sold to the poor for food. Yet Jesus said that not a single sparrow falls to the ground without our heavenly Father's knowing about it. He went on to say that we are much more important to God than birds and that he will always provide for our needs (Matthew 10:29-31).

What bird lays its eggs right on the bare ground?

The ostrich. The hot desert sun incubates the eggs during the day (Job 39:13-18).

Camels

One Hump or Two?

The camels mentioned in the Bible (such as in Genesis 24:61-64) were Arabian camels—the kind with one hump. Two-humped camels, also known as Bactrian camels, are found mostly in Asia. Arabian camels live in the hot deserts of the Middle East, while Bactrian camels live in colder climates.

When most people think of Bible lands, they think of camels. And for good reason! Camels made it possible to travel across hot, dry deserts. Without them it would have been hard to make long land journeys. Even today the Bedouin tribes of nomads (wanderers) depend on the unique abilities of camels.

Camels were the largest animals that most people in Bible times saw. Jesus used the camel to show how hard it is for someone who loves money to trust God. He said, "It is easier for a camel to go through the eye of a needle than for a rich man to enter the Kingdom of God!" (Matthew 19:24).

Ship of the Desert

Camels are custom-made for life in the dry, harsh conditions of Bible lands. Their nostrils can close to filter out blowing sand. Long eyelashes protect their eyes. When sand gets past the eyelashes, their transparent eyelids can wipe it away like windshield wipers. A strong digestive system helps camels get the most out of poor-quality desert plants. The hump is a reserve of fat that camels can draw from when food is in short supply. If necessary, camels can go three or four days without water. And a camel can lose a third of its body water without harm. All of these special abilities made camels the number-one choice for transportation through the desert (Genesis 37:25).

All-purpose Animals

Camels had many uses in Bible times.

- *Hauling.* A camel could carry as much as 400 pounds (180 kilograms) of baggage.
- *Cloth.* In winter, camels often grew a thicker coat of hair that could be shorn like sheep's wool in the springtime. (John the Baptist's clothes were made of camel's hair; Matthew 3:4.)
- *Milk.* Camels were also a source of milk. The Hebrews did not eat camel meat because it was "unclean" (Leviticus 11:4).
- *Shopping.* Camels were the Israelites' shopping malls. Merchants often used them to carry their wares from town to town. When merchants traveled together, they formed caravans. Caravans could have as many as 1,500 camels in them. A caravan of camels brought the Queen of Sheba's gifts to Israel in King Solomon's day (1 Kings 10:2).

Water Tank

When camels are thirsty, such as after a week-long journey, they can drink as much as 25 gallons (95 liters) of water in ten minutes. Each of their three stomachs can hold five gallons (19 liters) of water. Isaac's servant knew this when he brought his ten thirsty camels to the well in Nahor's village. When Rebekah drew water for him and all his camels "until they had enough" (Genesis 24:20), he knew she was an extraordinary young woman!

From the East

Did three wise men ride camels when they followed the star to the baby Jesus? The Bible tells about the wise men and the star, but it does not say how many wise men came or what they rode (Matthew 2:1-12).

Who lost 3000 camels but gained 6000 more?

Job. Read the story in Job 1:1-3, 17; 42:12.

Dreams & Visions

Creatures with four faces, two wings, and feet like cows? A dragon with seven heads and ten horns? Locusts with breastplates and golden crowns? What are these strange creatures that appear in the dreams and visions of certain men in the Bible? What did Daniel's, Ezekiel's, and John's visions mean?

God often used dreams and visions to tell people what was going to happen. Sometimes the Bible explains a dream or vision. At other times, history shows us what the dream or vision was all about. But sometimes we just don't understand the meaning. That's because some of the dreams and visions in the Bible are about things that haven't happened yet! The prophet Daniel wrote, "Gabriel started toward me. But as he approached, I was too frightened to stand, and fell down with my face to the ground. 'Son of man,' he said, 'you must understand that the events you have seen in your vision will not take place until the end times come' " (Daniel 8:17).

Four Strange Animals

The prophet Daniel had visions about strange animals. In one vision, he saw four animals rising out of the ocean. The first was like a lion with eagle's wings. In the dream, the creature's wings were pulled off, and it was left to stand on two legs. The second animal was like a bear ready to strike. The third was like a leopard with wings and four heads. The fourth creature was too terrible for Daniel to describe, but it was much more powerful than the others. It tore victims apart with its terrible iron teeth and crushed others with its feet. Later, this terrible animal was killed and its body burned because of its defiance of God. An angel told Daniel that the animals stood for four kings who would rule the earth (Daniel 7:1-27).

A Goat and a Ram

Daniel had another vision about a goat charging and trampling a ram. Daniel did not know what these animals stood for. Today we know that the animals represent two major world empires: the ram represents Medo-Persia and the goat represents Greece (Daniel 8:1-26).

Hungry Cows

With God's help, Joseph interpreted a dream that got him out of prison. Pharaoh had dreamed that seven fat cows came up out of the Nile River and began grazing in the grass. Suddenly, seven skinny cows came up out of the river and ate the fat ones (Genesis 41:1-4). God used this dream and Joseph's interpretation to show his plan for Egypt.

Amazing Animals

The book of Revelation is probably the most amazing and puzzling book in the Bible. Animals are very important symbols in John's vision. Here is a list of some of the creatures he saw and what they mean:

The Lion and the Lamb. Both are Jesus. Jesus is called the Lion of the Tribe of Judah (see Revelation 5:5). He is also called the Lamb who had been slaughtered (verse 6). This Lamb had seven horns and seven eyes!

The Four Living Beings. These beings stood at the four sides of God's throne (Revelation 4:6-8). One was like a lion, another like an ox, the third like a man, and the fourth like a flying eagle. These angelic creatures show us that God is kingly, faithful, intelligent, and all-powerful. Ezekiel also saw a vision of four winged beings (Ezekiel 1:5-14).

The Horses. With heads like lions and mouths that breathed fire, these horses were terrifying. Their tails were like serpents' heads; unlike ordinary horses, they bit and left fatal wounds, killing one-third of all people on earth (Revelation 9:13-19).

The Dragon. It was red and had seven heads and ten horns, with a crown on each head (Revelation 12:1-17). Thrown out of heaven by Michael and his angels, the Dragon—also known as the devil— began to attack God's people.

The Creatures. The Creature from the sea was an animal like a leopard but with bear's feet and a lion's mouth (Revelation 13:1-4). The Creature from the earth had two little horns like a lamb but a voice like the Dragon's (Revelation 13:11). Fortunately, these creatures will be defeated and thrown into the Lake of Fire (Revelation 19:19-21).

Who dreamed God told him to eat snakes?

The apostle Peter (Acts 10:9-16).

Dogs

Most dogs in ancient Israel were wild, just like their relatives the wolves, foxes, jackals, and hyenas. Job had some sheepdogs (Job 30:1), but this was unusual. Most dogs roamed the streets and fought over garbage outside the city walls. Wild dogs preyed on helpless herds of sheep and goats, especially at night. For these reasons the Israelites hated and feared dogs. They rarely, if ever, associated dogs with loyalty or companionship. This is why they had sayings such as, "As a dog returns to his vomit, so a fool repeats his folly" (Proverbs 26:11).

Striped Hyena

Hyenas

Hyenas look like dogs but have a unique howl that sounds like high-pitched laughing. They have large heads and powerful jaws, and they can easily crush cattle bones. Hyenas can devour dead animals whole without leaving a trace. They tear their victims apart. This is what they did to Jezebel's body (2 Kings 9:36). Hyenas are not as common in Palestine today as they once were. Still, there are enough of them in some areas that it is wise to bury corpses deep in the ground.

Watch Out for Wolves!

A "wolf in sheep's clothing" is someone dangerous who tries to fool others by appearing friendly. Jesus warned against hypocritical religious leaders: "Beware of false teachers who come disguised as harmless sheep, but are wolves and will tear you apart" (Matthew 7:15).

Dirty Dogs

Dogs, and also jackals and hyenas, were forbidden as food (Leviticus 11:26-28). They fed on corpses and even dug up recently buried bodies. This made them a health risk—a good reason for people to avoid them. In Israel, to call someone a "dog" was a real insult.

Fennec Fox

Foxes

In ancient times, as today, the fox was known for being sly. Three species are familiar to Egypt and Palestine: the red fox, the desert fox, and the fennec fox. These animals are active at night and spend most of the daytime in holes in the ground (as Jesus pointed out in Matthew 8:20). They hunt alone, eating everything from worms to small animals to vegetables, but they seem to especially enjoy grapes. Jesus called Herod "that fox," probably because he could not be trusted (Luke 13:32).

Jackals

The Hebrew word for "fox" can also mean "jackal." Jackals travel in packs, while foxes travel alone. This makes some people think that the animals Samson caught may have been jackals. He captured three hundred of them, tied torches to their tails, and set them loose in his enemies' field. The crops caught fire and were destroyed. (See the story in Judges 15:1-5.)

Hungry Puppies

Jesus once used the word *dog* to refer to people. He had been visited by a foreign woman who wanted him to heal her sick daughter. When she asked for Jesus' help, he replied: "It doesn't seem right to take bread from the children and throw it to the dogs." He knew the religious leaders thought of foreigners as "dogs" who didn't deserve God's blessings. Jesus used these words to show the leaders' wrong attitude. The woman replied, "Even the puppies beneath the table are permitted to eat the crumbs that fall" (Matthew 15:26-27). She didn't care what people called her; she just wanted God to bless her daughter. What was Jesus' response to this foreign woman who believed in God's power? "Woman . . . your faith is large, and your request is granted." Her daughter was healed right then.

Who did King David say should howl like dogs?

Evil people (Psalm 59:14-15).

Lizards

Lizards look just like miniature dinosaurs. They were very common in the lands of the Bible. The Jewish people had at least seven names for lizards. But lizards are seldom mentioned in the Bible. The Israelites generally avoided lizards because they weren't allowed to eat them: "These are the forbidden small animals which scurry about your feet or crawl upon the ground: the mole, the rat, the great lizard, the gecko, the mouse, the lizard, the snail, the chameleon" (Leviticus 11:29-30). One proverb about lizards says they are small but unusually wise "because they are easy to catch and kill, yet are found even in king's palaces" (Proverbs 30:28).

House Gecko

Geckos

It probably was quite common for an Israelite woman to see a lizard running up a wall in her home! Geckos were especially good at this. They have sticky pads on their toes (too small to be seen) that allow them to cling to walls and ceilings.

Land Monitor

Monitors

Land monitors (or monitor lizards) were common in Palestine. Unlike geckos, monitors were not a nuisance to people because they normally lived in the desert and stayed away from civilized areas. Monitors grow up to five feet (1.5 meters) long and have sharp teeth and long tails. Water monitors, a related species, can grow even larger.

Chameleons: Masters of Disguise

Lizards are good at survival in the desert. Chameleons avoid danger by changing color to match their surroundings. Certain other kinds of lizards can do this, too. A chameleon's eyes are on opposite sides of its head, and these eyes move independently. Like most other lizards, chameleons eat insects. A chameleon can fling out its tongue—which is as long as its body—with blinding speed and capture prey on its sticky tip.

Jackson's Chameleon

Insect Eaters

Lizards helped people by eating insects that would otherwise infest homes and eat crops.

W̲h̲a̲t̲ ̲w̲o̲u̲l̲d̲ ̲a̲n̲ ̲I̲s̲r̲a̲e̲l̲i̲t̲e̲
h̲a̲v̲e̲ ̲t̲o̲ ̲d̲o̲ ̲i̲f̲ ̲h̲e̲ ̲f̲o̲u̲n̲d̲ ̲a̲ ̲d̲e̲a̲d̲
l̲i̲z̲a̲r̲d̲ ̲i̲n̲ ̲t̲h̲e̲ ̲c̲o̲o̲k̲i̲e̲ ̲j̲a̲r̲?̲

Break the jar (Leviticus 11:33).

Extraordinary Animals

The Israelites rarely saw animals like bears, elephants, and apes. But they certainly knew about them. They feared the bears that lived in the forests. They carved the precious imported ivory of African elephants. And they knew about the exotic apes and monkeys owned by Solomon. God used some extraordinary animals to show Job how foolish it is to question him. These animals are among the ones God describes in Job 38–41:

- lions
- ostriches
- eagles
- hippopotami
- crocodiles

Brown Bears

The Big, Bad Bears

An extremely dangerous animal is "a mother bear who has been robbed of her cubs" (2 Samuel 17:8). Bears were feared even more than lions because bears were more unpredictable and more deadly when provoked. Though many people think that bears are only meat-eaters, they actually eat both plants and animals (they're omnivorous). Most of the year bears eat wild fruits and berries. They are most likely to attack livestock in winter when fruit is scarce. The only time they might attack people is when they feel threatened. One time, though, two female bears killed forty-two young people because they mocked Elisha, a prophet of God (2 Kings 2:23-24).

Lion-tailed Macaques

Migrating Monkeys

Solomon imported animals for his zoo from faraway lands such as Africa and India (1 Kings 10:22). The "apes" he imported could have been macaques or langurs from southern India, or baboons or vervet monkeys from northeastern Africa. Pictures of the Indian monkeys have been found on Assyrian monuments dating from the time of Solomon. This shows that his interest in animals was a serious hobby! (See 1 Kings 4:33.)

Ivory Treasures

Ivory comes from elephant tusks. It is very expensive. King Solomon's throne was inlaid with ivory and overlaid with gold (2 Chronicles 9:17).

These ivory animals are almost 3000 years old.

W̲ho caught bears and lions by the jaw and clubbed them to death?

David, while guarding his father's sheep (1 Samuel 17:34-36).

Horses

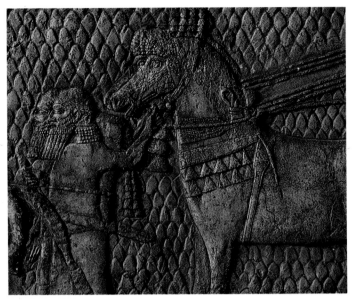

Babylonian War Horse

Powerful yet gentle, horses have served humans for thousands of years. They were used in war long before they were used in farming. In Bible times an army's strength was measured by how many horses it had (Isaiah 2:7).

Because horses were so strong, the Israelites were often tempted to depend on them too much for protection. Sometimes the Israelites trusted in horses more than they trusted in God. The Bible warns against this. "A war horse is a poor risk for winning victories—it is strong but it cannot save" (Psalm 33:17).

Army Transport

Few families in Israel owned horses. They didn't need horses because they used donkeys and camels for transportation. Only kings and generals needed horses, which they used in their armies. Israel's powerful enemies, Egypt and Assyria, owned many horses.

Symbols of War

In the book of Revelation, horses are used as symbols of power and war. You can read about the white horse, the red horse, the black horse, and the pale horse (chapter 6); the war horses with scorpions' tails (chapter 9); and the white horse carrying the King of kings, who defeated the beast and all the world's armies (chapter 19).

Defense Arsenal

The Israelites didn't always listen to God's warnings against trusting in horses. King David said it was better to trust in the Lord than in chariots and horses (Psalm 20:7). Yet David also bought horses for Israel's defense. So did his son King Solomon, who "owned forty thousand chariot horses" (1 Kings 4:26).

Arabian Horses

Chariots

Horses were used to pull chariots. Originally chariots were four-wheeled carriages. Later the Egyptians made the two-wheeled version popular. This was the kind Joseph rode (see Genesis 46:29).

War chariots were:

- top-of-the-line military equipment, the tanks of the ancient world
- pulled by two horses
- usually five feet (1.5 meters) across
- lightweight so horses could run at top speed
- manned by charioteers armed with spears and bows and arrows

What did Joshua do with the Canaanite horses his soldiers captured?

He had the tendons in their legs cut so they couldn't run (Joshua 11:6-9).

27

Flying Pests

Butterflies are insects, and they are beautiful. Bees are insects, and they give honey. Frogs and mice and other small animals like insects because they are tasty snacks. But usually when we think of insects, we think of flying pests. The Bible tells of damage from grasshoppers, gnats, hornets, moths, lice, flies, and other insects. It mentions how these insects sting, annoy, bite, carry disease, and destroy things such as clothing or crops. Bees and hornets are mentioned both because they sting (Deuteronomy 1:44; 7:20) and because they produce honey (Judges 14:8). But the Bible has only good things to say about ants (Proverbs 6:6)!

The Bible mentions grasshoppers (or locusts) 56 times. One of the words for grasshopper means "swallow up" or "destroy." They earned this name from their ability to completely strip vegetation. Grasshoppers can make a field of ripe grain bare, until it looks as if nothing had been planted there.

Bugs in the Water
Israelites strained their drinking water through cloth to get the insects out. Jesus pointed out that some people avoid little sins while ignoring big ones: "You strain out a gnat and swallow a camel" (Matthew 23:24).

Gnat

Honeybee

Wasp

Hornet

Stinging Insects

Bees, wasps, and hornets were well known to the people of Bible lands. Though bees could be pests, the honey they made was important because it was the only sweetener most people could get. Most honey was gathered from the combs of wild bees that nested in hollow trees or rocky holes (or other places, as mentioned in Judges 14:8-9). Hornets in the Bible lands were usually more aggressive than the kinds we know. The Lord sent hornets to clear the Promised Land of nations under God's judgment (Joshua 24:12). Some other ancient documents describe how entire cities had to flee because of invasions of short-tempered hornets.

An Israelite Ceramic Moth

Moths

Today, as in Bible times, moths are disliked because they eat fabric. Actually, their caterpillar larvae, not adult moths themselves, do the damage. Female moths lay their eggs on clothing that has been stored away. When these eggs hatch, the caterpillars eat the fabric until they are big enough to become moths. Jesus warned against becoming attached to things that moths can destroy (Matthew 6:19-20).

Emperor Moth

What prophet ate a steady diet of grass-hoppers and wild honey?

John the Baptist (John 3:4).

29

Donkeys & Mules

Jesus Rides into Jerusalem

Today we ride in cars and trucks. In Bible times people rode donkeys. Camels, like big trucks, carried heavy loads long distances. Donkeys, like cars, were available to most people for transportation and hauling. Often donkeys carried loads larger than themselves.

A donkey had the privilege of carrying Jesus into the city of Jerusalem on Palm Sunday. "Jesus rode along on a young donkey, fulfilling the prophecy that said: 'Don't be afraid of your King, people of Israel, for he will come to you meekly, sitting on a donkey's colt!'" (John 12:14-15, quoting Zechariah 9:9).

Riding a Donkey

Almost all Hebrews rode donkeys. Riding a donkey was entirely different from riding a horse. Rather than using a saddle, the rider would place a straw pad over a thick cloth on the donkey's back. Then he or she would cover the straw with a carpet or strong cloth. The rider steered with a bridle but no bit. The good Samaritan was riding a donkey when he came across the injured man (Luke 10:34).

Pickup Truck

The Israelites valued donkeys because they are surefooted and cheap to feed. The Hebrews used donkeys to haul loads, grind corn (by turning a millstone), and pull plows. If a person could afford to own only one animal, it was usually a donkey.

Donkey and Young

Donkey Facts

- Donkeys were some of the first tamed (or domesticated) animals in Bible lands.
- Usually brown or gray, donkeys generally have a stripe over the shoulders.
- Donkeys come in all sizes: some stand only three feet (1.5 meters) high, while others are as large as a full-grown horse.
- Donkeys usually sleep standing up.
- The noise a donkey makes is called "braying."

Wandering Donkeys

The Hebrews grazed their donkeys in open fields rather than fenced-in pens. Sometimes these donkeys wandered off, and the owners had to look for them. Saul hunted for his father's donkeys for three days without finding them. But God used Saul's search to lead him to the prophet Samuel, who anointed Saul king of Israel. (See the story in 1 Samuel 9:3-27.)

Mule Trivia

- A mule is the offspring of a donkey and a horse.
- Mules are larger than donkeys and often live longer than horses.
- Mules are strong animals that can be used for riding and transporting goods.
- There are many references to mules in the Old Testament. David and his sons had mules (2 Samuel 13:29). Absalom, David's rebellious son, was riding his mule when his hair became tangled in the branches of an oak tree (see 2 Samuel 18:9-17). When Solomon was anointed king of Israel, he rode on David's personal mule (1 Kings 1:32-40).
- Mules are stubborn. At times they plant their feet and refuse to do what their master says—often for no apparent reason! King David said, "Don't be like a senseless horse or mule that has to have a bit in its mouth to keep it in line!" (Psalm 32:9).

What donkey scolded its owner and got away with it?

Balaam's donkey. (See Numbers 22:21-38 for the whole story.)

Sacrifices

In Old Testament times, God required animal sacrifices for sin. Then Jesus made the greatest sacrifice of all—he died on the cross for us! Because of Jesus' death and resurrection, we no longer need animal sacrifices. That is why John the Baptist called Jesus "the Lamb of God, who takes away the world's sin!" (John 1:29).

Bull

Sheep

Goat

Dove

Pigeon

Flour

Kinds of Sacrifices

God listed which animals the Israelites were allowed to sacrifice. Oxen (cows and bulls), sheep (ewes and rams), goats, doves, and pigeons were allowed; other animals were not. The kind of animal used for a sacrifice depended on what the sacrifice was for and what a person could afford. For example, the "sin offering" required

- a young bull for the whole nation
- a male goat for a leader
- a female goat for a common person
- a dove or pigeon for a poor person
- a small amount of fine flour for a very poor person (Leviticus 4:1-13).

Missing the Point

People in Bible times sometimes missed the point of sacrifice. Killing an animal did not take away sin (Hebrews 10:8). The sacrifices were reminders of how costly sin is, but the sacrifices weren't magic. God wanted people to be sorry for their sin and obey him. The prophet Samuel said, "Has the Lord as much pleasure in your burnt offerings and sacrifices as in your obedience? . . . He is much more interested in your listening to him than in your offering the fat of rams to him" (1 Samuel 15:22).

Living Sacrifices

In the Bible, a "sacrifice" was something—usually an animal—that someone set apart to give to God. This usually was done by burning the sacrifice on an altar. When something was set apart in this way, it was considered *holy*. Because it was being given to God, anything used as a sacrifice was supposed to be the best, most nearly perfect thing available. For example, when a sheep was the sacrifice, it could not have any spots or imperfections.

Though we do not burn sacrifices on altars today, we can still set things apart to give to God. In fact, the apostle Paul wrote about the most wonderful "sacrifice" we can make: "I plead with you to give your bodies to God. Let them be a living sacrifice, holy—the kind he can accept" (Romans 12:1). Giving our bodies to God means living the way he wants us to live.

What happened to the meat of animals that were sacrificed?

Some was burned on the altar, some was given to the priests and Levites for food, and some was returned to those who brought the animal (Leviticus 7:1-21).

33

Snakes

The first animal story in the Bible involves a snake. Satan came to Eve in the form of a talking serpent. Eve and Adam believed Satan's lies. They brought sin into their own lives and into all of God's creation. The serpent was cursed and forced to crawl on its belly (Genesis 3:14-15).

Because of the story of Adam and Eve, snakes often are used to symbolize evil. Satan is called a serpent many times. "This great Dragon—the ancient serpent called the devil, or Satan, the one deceiving the whole world—was thrown down onto the earth with all his army" (Revelation 12:9).

Poison and Healing

Poisonous snakes attacked the people of Israel as they traveled in the wilderness (Numbers 21:4-6). Many people died, but some begged God for help. So he told Moses to make a brass serpent and raise it up on a pole where the people could see it. Those who looked at the serpent recovered from the snakebites (Numbers 21:7-9). Jesus said, "As Moses in the wilderness lifted up the bronze image of a serpent on a pole, even so I must be lifted up upon a pole [the cross], so that anyone who believes in me will have eternal life" (John 3:14-15).

Cobras: All Puffed Up

Israelites were familiar with cobras. Egyptian cobras eat rats and mice. When threatened, they puff up their necks. Cobras are deadlier than vipers or rattlesnakes. Their venom attacks the nervous system directly. Psalm 58:4-5 and Isaiah 11:8 may refer to cobras.

The Viper's Venom

The carpet viper is common in Middle Eastern deserts. Its venom takes several days to kill a person. It kills by destroying blood cells, blood vessels, and muscle tissue. The serpents that bit some Israelites on their way to the Promised Land were probably carpet vipers.

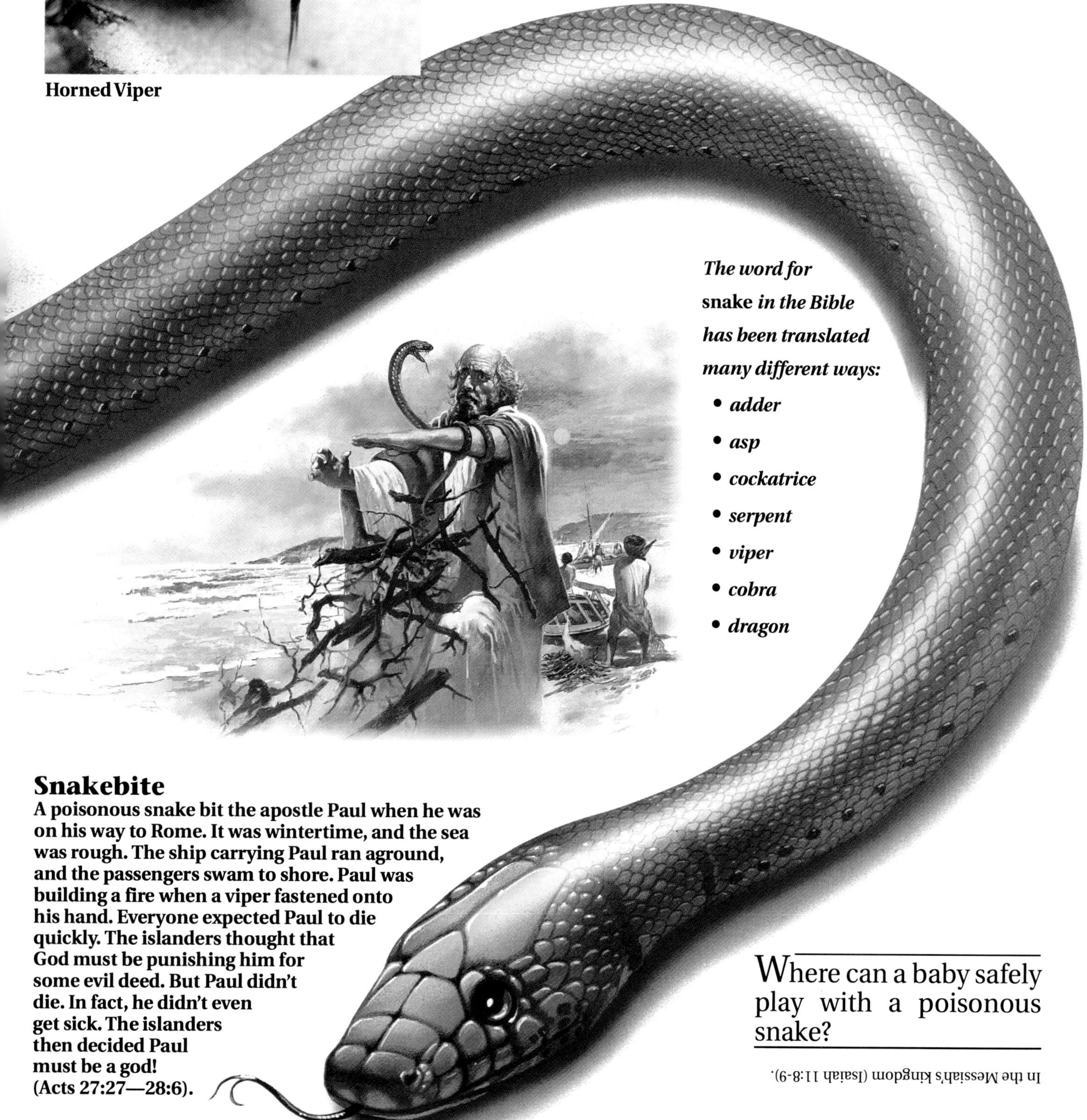

Horned Viper

The word for snake in the Bible has been translated many different ways:

- *adder*
- *asp*
- *cockatrice*
- *serpent*
- *viper*
- *cobra*
- *dragon*

Snakebite

A poisonous snake bit the apostle Paul when he was on his way to Rome. It was wintertime, and the sea was rough. The ship carrying Paul ran aground, and the passengers swam to shore. Paul was building a fire when a viper fastened onto his hand. Everyone expected Paul to die quickly. The islanders thought that God must be punishing him for some evil deed. But Paul didn't die. In fact, he didn't even get sick. The islanders then decided Paul must be a god! (Acts 27:27—28:6).

Where can a baby safely play with a poisonous snake?

In the Messiah's kingdom (Isaiah 11:8-9).

35

Cats

Cats come in many sizes and shapes, but all the Bible cats are large. Leopards, cheetahs, and lions were all familiar in Bible lands. When the Israelites were in Egypt, they would have seen many small cats as well.

Leopards are masters at stalking, catching, and swiftly killing their prey. Lions are just as dangerous. God used these dangerous animals to warn Israel of his judgment: "So I will come upon you like a lion, or a leopard lurking along the road" (Hosea 13:7).

Cheetah Cubs

Look Out for Leopards!

Leopards were extremely dangerous to the Israelite herds of sheep and goats. They were not as easily scared off as wild dogs. Shepherds would always look for sheep that had wandered off because sheep were prime targets for hungry leopards roaming the hills and forests. Leopards' stealth and speed made them even more effective hunters than their lion cousins. Leopards could hunt individual animals and take them almost completely by surprise. By contrast, lions hunted herds and often gave away their presence by roaring. Almost every time the Bible mentions leopards, it talks about how fierce and fast they are (Habakkuk 1:8; Hosea 13:7).

Sizing Up Cats

	Average height at shoulder	Average length including tail	Average weight
Tiger	5 ft (1.5 m)	14 ft (4.3 m)	500 lb (225 kg)
Lion	3 ft (90 cm)	9.5 ft (2.9 m)	400-500 lb (180-225 kg)
Leopard	2.5 ft (75 cm)	7 ft (2.1 m)	110 lb (50 kg)
Cheetah	2.5 ft (75 cm)	6 ft (1.8 m)	100 lb (45 kg)
Domestic Cat	1 ft (30 cm)	20-28 in (50-70 cm)	6-10 lb (2.7-4.5 kg)

Egyptian Cat Idol

Holy Cats!

God warned the Israelites against worshiping the gods of Egypt (Joshua 24:14). Egypt had many cat gods. Around 1580 B.C., while the Israelites were living in Egypt, a religious cult was formed to worship the cat goddess Bast (or Pasht). This goddess represented motherhood. Because cats were considered so special, the Egyptians treated them very well. It was illegal to harm cats in any way. When a cat of a wealthy family died, it was embalmed and made into a mummy just as humans were. Then it was placed in a tomb and grieved over just like a family member. Some museums of natural history have cat mummies on display. A few cat mummies have even been discovered with mouse mummies nearby.

The prophet Jeremiah once said that it's as hard for an evil person to do good as it is for . . .

. . . a leopard to change its spots (Jeremiah 13:23).

Fish

In Bible times fishing was a common occupation. Most people ate fish because meat was expensive. Several of the disciples whom Jesus called were fishermen. Many stories about Jesus involved fishing (Mark 7:31-37; John 6:1-13). Jesus often compared working with him to fishing: "Come along with me and I will show you how to fish for the souls of men!" (Matthew 4:19).

School of Barracuda

Kinds of Fish

In spite of the great numbers of fish caught by the ancient Israelites, the Bible never mentions any specific kind of fish! Edible saltwater fish probably included mackerel, barracuda, herring, and shad. These fish came from the Mediterranean Sea. (Fish don't live in the Dead Sea. The water there is too salty for most marine life.) Lakes and streams, such as the Sea of Galilee and the Jordan River, provided freshwater favorites, such as St. Peter's fish and perch.

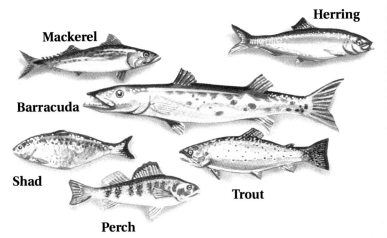

Mackerel
Herring
Barracuda
Shad
Trout
Perch

Swallowed by a Fish

When the prophet Jonah tried to run away from God, he was swallowed by "a great fish" (Jonah 1:17). He spent three days and three nights inside the fish before it spit him up on the beach. Killer whales have been known to swallow seals and dolphins. It may have been such a whale that swallowed Jonah. Or it may have been an actual fish, much bigger than any fish known today.

Miracle Fish

On two separate occasions, Jesus multiplied fish miraculously to feed a hungry crowd. The story of the feeding of the 5,000 is in Matthew 14:13-21, and the feeding of the 4,000 is in Matthew 15:32-39.

Fish for Breakfast

One night after the death and resurrection of Jesus, some of the disciples went fishing. Jesus met them on the shore at dawn and made a breakfast of bread and fish for them (John 21:10-13).

Fishing Nets

The ways of fishing in the Sea of Galilee haven't changed much since Bible times. Often a net was used. It was usually circular, with weights around the outside edges. The weights would sink to the bottom, trapping the fish. The fisherman would then pull a cord attached to the center, drawing the edges of the net together as it rose to the surface. Jesus' disciples were fishing this way when he told them to throw their net over to the other side of the boat to catch fish (John 21:4-6).

ICHTHUS

The fish became a Christian symbol soon after Jesus' death and resurrection. When Christianity started to spread, some people didn't like this new religion. They persecuted the new Christians so much that some Christians invented secret codes so they could recognize one another. They used the Greek word *ichthus*, which means "fish":

- **Iesous** Jesus
- **Christos** Christ
- **Theou** of God
- **Uios** Son
- **Soter** Savior

What fish paid taxes?

The fish Jesus told Peter to catch (Matthew 17:24-27).

Dragons & Monsters

Perhaps you've heard there are unicorns in the Bible—but you haven't been able to find any! The Hebrew word for "wild ox" was translated "unicorn" in the King James Version. Even though unicorns have been popular for many years in myths, legends, and stories, no evidence of their existence has ever been found.

People who first translated the Bible into English did not know what animals existed in the Middle East. When they read animal names they did not recognize, they gave them names like unicorn, leviathan, behemoth, and sea monster. With a better understanding of the Bible languages, we now know what many (but not all) of these difficult words probably meant.

How Some Difficult Words Have Been Translated

	KJV	NIV	TLB	NASB	NRSV
Numbers 23:22	unicorn	wild ox	wild ox	wild ox	wild ox
Job 40:15	behemoth	behemoth	hippo-potamus	Behemoth	Behemoth
Job 41:1	leviathan	leviathan	crocodile	Leviathan	Leviathan
Psalm 91:13	dragon	serpent	poisonous snake	serpent	serpent
Lamentations 4:3	sea monster	jackal	jackal	jackal	jackal

[King James Version, New International Version, *The Living Bible*, *New American Standard Bible*, and New Revised Standard Version]

Leviathan

There are many references to "leviathan" in the Bible, but its exact meaning is unclear. Some references make it sound like a crocodile: "Can you catch a [leviathan] with a hook and line? Or put a noose around his tongue? Can you tie him with a rope through the nose, or pierce his jaw with a spike? . . . Can you make a pet of him like a bird? . . . If you lay your hand upon him, you will long remember the battle that ensues, and you will never try it again!" (Job 41:1-8). Other parts of the Bible describe leviathan as a creature God made to play in the sea (Psalm 104:26, KJV), which makes it sound more like a porpoise or a whale. Sometimes Hebrew words can refer to more than one kind of animal, and so "leviathan" may mean a crocodile, a porpoise, a whale, or some other large animal.

Hippopotamus

Behemoth

"Behemoth" was some kind of large beast that had great strength. For that reason, it often is translated "hippopotamus." Crocodiles and elephants also have been suggested because the behemoth had a large tail (Job 40:17) and was not frightened by a raging river (Job 40:23).

Dragons

Some Bible translations are full of dragons! In the King James Version, the Hebrew words *tannim* and *tannin* were both translated "dragon." Today *tannim* is considered to refer to a jackal (a kind of wild dog related to the wolf) rather than a dragon. *Tannin* refers to dragons seen in visions (such as in Revelation 12:1-17).

<u>**W**hy did God create the sea monster?</u>

To frolic (play) in the sea. (Psalm 104:26).

Sheep

Sheep are mentioned at least 750 times in the Bible. God often compared his people to sheep. (Psalm 100:3 is an example.) In some ways we all act like sheep. "We—every one of us—have strayed away like sheep! We left God's paths to follow our own" (Isaiah 53:6).

The most important sheep in the Bible is a lamb—God's Lamb, Jesus. In Old Testament times, sheep often were sacrificed for sins. Jesus, God's Son, sacrificed himself for our sins. When John the Baptist saw Jesus, he said, "Look! There is the Lamb of God who takes away the world's sin!" (John 1:29).

Broadtail Sheep

Sheep have been tamed (or domesticated) in many countries for thousands of years. In ancient Israel, the broadtail sheep was the most common breed. The tail had delicious meat. Wild animals often attacked these sheep because they were easy and tasty prey.

Sheep Need Protection

Sheep are gentle creatures. They are easily led from pasture to pasture, where they happily munch on grass. Yet their gentle nature makes them easy targets for predators like wolves and lions. Sheep have little ability to defend themselves. They depend totally on their shepherds for protection. Also, they can easily get separated from the herd and not find their way home. It takes a lot of time and attention to care for a flock of sheep. Shepherds in the Bible include Jacob (Genesis 46:28–47:6), David (1 Samuel 17:20-37), and Amos (Amos 1:1). King David said, "The Lord is my shepherd" (Psalm 23:1), and Jesus called himself "the Good Shepherd" (John 10:1-21).

The Master's Voice

Shepherds often talked to their sheep. Some, like David, even sang to them. Over time, sheep learn to recognize their shepherd's voice, much the way dogs and cats learn their master's voice. They do not respond to a stranger's voice. Jesus said his sheep—meaning his followers—hear and respond to his voice (John 10:4-5).

Food and Clothing

Sheep were important to the everyday lives of the Jewish people. Wool was used in clothing (Proverbs 31:13), and sheepskins were all some people had to wear (Hebrews 11:37). Sheep also were a source of meat for food and sacrifices.

Sheep Drinking

The Sheepfold

A sheepfold was a fenced-off place where sheep could be kept safe during the night. Built with high stone walls, it offered protection from wild beasts and thieves. Late in the day, shepherds would guide their animals into the pen through the gate. The shepherds would sleep in front of the entrance until daybreak. Jesus said, "I am the Gate for the sheep" (John 10:7).

Wool

- Sheep in Bible times produced about two pounds (one kilogram) of wool a year.
- Sheep today produce more than twice as much wool, thanks to careful breeding.
- Wool is not hair. Unlike hair, wool has scales of overlapping plates.

Who is called both a lion and a lamb?

Jesus, while standing before the 24 elders (Revelation 5:5-8).

Animal Plagues

"Go back again to Pharaoh and tell him that he *must* let the people of Israel go," God told Moses (Exodus 6:11). Moses went, but Pharaoh wouldn't listen. It took ten plagues to change his mind.

Animals were involved in all ten of the plagues. Sometimes they were victims of the plagues. Sometimes they were part of the plagues themselves. Fish, cattle, camels, donkeys, and other livestock suffered and died because Pharaoh wouldn't listen. Frogs, lice, flies, and grasshoppers visited the Egyptians in huge, thick swarms. The plagues did not directly affect the Israelites. Only the Egyptians suffered.

First plague—water to blood
(Exodus 7:14-24)
The Nile River was the Egyptian lifeline. It gave the people fish, fresh water, and fertile silt for their farmland when it flooded. When the Nile turned to blood, all the fish died, and the water became too polluted to drink.

Second plague—hordes of frogs *(Exodus 8:1-15)*
Frogs were plentiful in Egypt along the banks of the Nile. During flood season, they would rapidly multiply. This time the frogs became so numerous that they entered every house in Egypt. But at Moses' command, frogs away from the river quickly died, rotting by the millions. Imagine having hundreds of dead frogs rotting in your house—even in your bed! That's what happened to the Egyptians when Pharaoh refused to listen to Moses.

Imagine being nibbled to death by flies! See the fourth plague for details . . .

Third plague—lice *(Exodus 8:16-19)*

The word for the insects in the third plague has been translated "lice" or "gnats." Either of these insects would have caused incredible misery as they infested Egypt by the millions.

Fourth plague—swarms of flies *(Exodus 8:20-32)*

The flies in this plague weren't just bothersome house flies, but swarms of stinging sand flies. These flies bit people and animals, spreading disease. Like the frogs, the flies infested every home in Egypt.

Fifth plague—death of livestock *(Exodus 9:1-7)*

Most of Egypt's cattle, horses, donkeys, camels, flocks, and herds died. This greatly hurt the Egyptians because they depended on their livestock for food, transportation, milk, and labor.

Sixth plague—boils *(Exodus 9:8-12)*

Boils are painful sores on the skin. Any animals left alive from the fifth plague suffered from these sores just as the people did.

Seventh plague—thunder and hail *(Exodus 9:13-35)*

Hail results when rain is blown back up into the colder upper atmosphere by updrafts. It freezes into snowball-like chunks and then falls again to the earth. Large hailstones can damage crops and harm animals and people. The hailstones that fell on Egypt killed all the animals left outside and unprotected.

Eighth plague—devouring grasshoppers *(Exodus 10:1-20)*

Grasshoppers (or locusts) are leaf-eating insects that, in large numbers, can eat whole fields of crops in a very short time. There is no way to predict grasshopper storms because they are usually carried by strong winds, sometimes as far as 100 miles (160 km).

Ninth plague—three days of darkness *(Exodus 10:21-29)*

During this time, the people of Egypt could not see to walk around because of the darkness.

Tenth plague—Egypt's firstborn die *(Exodus 12:29-30)*

Egypt's surviving animals suffered this tragedy just as the Egyptians themselves did. The Egyptians were sad that these animals died. But Pharaoh didn't let the Israelites go until all the firstborn sons in Egypt died. When he finally relented, he said, "Leave us. . . . Take your flocks and herds and be gone" (Exodus 12:31-32).

Which plagues made people itch?

The third (lice), fourth (flies), and sixth (boils).

45

Birds of Prey

Birds of prey and scavenger birds in the Bible include eagles, owls, vultures, hawks, cormorants, and ravens. These birds either hunt their food or eat animals killed in other ways. Many birds of prey are used as symbols in the Bible. For example, eagles represent God's power (Isaiah 40:31). Owls and ravens are signs of God's judgment (Isaiah 34:11-15).

Cape Eagle Owl

Owl Lore

Owls common to the Bible lands include the great owl (or eagle owl), screech owl, short-eared owl, long-eared owl, little owl, tawny owl, fisher owl, and desert owl. Owls helped the Israelite farmers by hunting rats, mice, and other rodents that damaged crops. Unlike other birds, which have eyes on the sides of their head, owls have both eyes in front of their head. They can turn their heads so far, though, that they have no trouble seeing all that is happening around them. Their keen night vision enables them to do most of their hunting at night.

The Bone Breaker

One kind of vulture was the ossifrage (also called lammergeier and bearded vulture). The name literally means "bone breaker." Ossifrages often shatter the bones of dead animals by dropping them from great heights in order to eat the marrow, which is found inside the bone.

An Ossifrage

The Mighty Eagle

The Bible uses eagles to illustrate many things:

- God's judgment, like an eagle swooping down on its prey (Deuteronomy 28:49; 32:11-12)
- God's care, like a mother eagle caring for her eaglets until they learn to fly (Deuteronomy 32:11)
- Pride, because eagles live high above everyone else (Jeremiah 49:16)

Golden Eagle

Scavengers

Vultures and ravens are scavenger birds rather than birds of prey. God used ravens to gather food for the prophet Elijah while he was hiding from his enemies (1 Kings 17:1-7). When vultures see a dead body, they gather around it and eat. Jesus said his second coming would be as plain to see as vultures gathering for a meal (Matthew 24:28).

What bird of prey cried out loudly, "Woe, woe, woe"?

An eagle (Revelation 8:13).

47

Animals That Run and Hide

While some animals were known in Bible lands for their swiftness of attack, other animals were known for their swiftness of escape. They stayed safe by running or by hiding where none of their enemies could find them.

The Bible writers admired these animals for their ability to avoid danger. Anyone who was exceptionally fast was "like a deer that escapes from a hunter" (Proverbs 6:5). And cliff badgers were thought to be unusually wise little animals because they could "protect themselves by living among the rocks" (Proverbs 30:26).

Deer

The kind of deer the Israelites admired, wrote about, and hunted was probably the fallow deer or roe deer (also called the hart). These deer were an important source of food for the Israelites. Esau probably hunted them (Genesis 25:27), and King Solomon had them on his daily menu (1 Kings 4:23). Because of the speed of the deer, the Israelites had to use nets to trap them.

Deer

Fallow Deer

Gazelles: Bible Speedsters

The gazelle is often used as a symbol of speed (see Song of Solomon 2:9, 17; 8:14). This is not surprising—a gazelle can run at speeds of up to forty miles an hour!

You Dirty Rat!

Rats and mice did a lot of damage to crops in the field, and they carried fleas that could spread serious diseases such as bubonic plague. The Philistines made five gold rats in an attempt to find forgiveness for taking the Ark of God (1 Samuel 6:4-18).

Rock Badgers

Rock badgers, also called coneys or cliff badgers, look like big guinea pigs. They live in the steep cliffs and rocks of the hillsides. Their feet have pads that allow them to climb on most rocky surfaces with ease. They live in colonies and post guards. Rock badgers are mentioned in both Psalms and Proverbs (Psalm 104:18; Proverbs 30:26).

Survival

Deer in Bible lands have to survive harsh desert conditions. Just as water is very important for deer, God is important for humans. David wrote, "As the deer pants for water, so I long for you, O God" (Psalm 42:1).

Incredible Animals

Some of the smaller animals common to Palestine are mentioned in the Bible as animals that the Israelites were not allowed to eat (Leviticus 11:4-7, 26-30). Among these are mole-rats, hares, rock (or cliff) badgers, rats, and mice. Mole-rats are completely blind gopherlike creatures that make underground tunnels. Farmers dislike them because they damage crops. Hares look like large rabbits.

The Bible says that hares chew the cud (Leviticus 11:6). Instead of rechewing what's in their stomach, as cows do, hares eat one kind of their droppings. This enables them to get the most nutrition from food that is hard to digest, just as cows do.

Which animals that run and hide were the Israelites allowed to eat—if they could catch them?

The ones with hooves (Deuteronomy 14:4-5).

Amazing Animal Stories

A serpent that lied (Genesis 3:1-14); a ram that saved a boy's life (Genesis 22:1-14); a staff that became a snake (Exodus 7:1-14); flaming horses that flew (2 Kings 2:1-11); a fish that swallowed a man alive (Jonah 1:1–2:10); a worm that taught a lesson (Jonah 4:1-11); a fish that paid taxes (Matthew 17:25-27); an untamed donkey ridden by a King (Luke 19:28-38); a beast with seven heads that will trick the world (Revelation 17:3-14). These are just some of the unforgettable animal stories in the Bible. Here are some more.

Polite Lions

Because Daniel was very good at his job, his coworkers became jealous of him. To get him in trouble, they got King Darius to make a law against praying. When Daniel prayed anyway, he was thrown into a den of lions. But the hungry lions held back from even touching Daniel because God had sent an angel to protect him. Daniel's jealous enemies were thrown into the den a short time later, and the lions tore them apart before their bodies even hit the ground. (See the story in Daniel 6:1-27.)

An Animal Boat Cruise

Soon after the world began, people became so evil that God decided to destroy everyone except one good man, Noah, and his family. God told Noah to build a boat (or ark) large enough to carry a pair of every land-dwelling animal on earth. This ark was as long as one and a half football fields, stood about four stories high, and had three levels—just enough space for all the passengers and their food. The ark's passengers were the only ones to survive the flood that covered the whole world. (See the story in Genesis 6:9–8:22.)

Bird Waiters

God used ravens to help his prophet Elijah survive a drought. Elijah was a prophet sent to tell the wicked King Ahab to turn away from his worship of Baal. As punishment for Ahab's evil, no rain had fallen for several years. God told his prophet to drink water from Cherith Brook and wait for the ravens to bring food. Just as God promised, the birds brought Elijah meat and bread each morning and evening. (See the story in 1 Kings 17:1-6.)

Noah took one pair of most kinds of animals on the ark. What kinds did he take *seven* pairs of?

Those animals needed for eating and for sacrifice (Genesis 7:2-3).

A Talking Donkey

A king named Balak once offered a bribe to the prophet Balaam to curse the Israelites, Balak's enemies. God sent an angel to stop Balaam. Balaam's donkey saw the angel, but Balaam didn't. Each time the donkey tried to stop Balaam from crossing the angel's path, Balaam would beat the donkey to make it obey him. Finally the donkey spoke and told Balaam about the angel. Then Balaam too saw the angel. (See the story in Numbers 22:21-34.)

Pigs

Today pigs are a normal part of life. Some people even keep them as pets. But Israelites wanted nothing to do with pigs. Their laws did not allow them to eat pig meat. Pigs were not used as sacrifices. Israelites did not raise pigs. They did not even want to look at pigs. If for some reason they had to get rid of a dead pig, they washed all their clothes. Pigs could even be dangerous. Jesus said, "Don't give pearls to swine! They will trample the pearls and turn and attack you" (Matthew 7:6).

Killer Worms

Today, as in Bible times, pigs often carry tiny worms inside them such as the trichina or the tapeworm. If a person eats pork (pig meat) infected with these worms, he or she can become very sick or even die. That's why pork must be cooked completely before it is served. Because the Israelites were not allowed to eat pig meat, they did not have to worry about this (Leviticus 11:7).

Pig Stampede

Jesus once used a herd of pigs to demonstrate his power to the Gentiles (non-Jewish people). Jesus had cast thousands of demons out of a man, and the demons begged Jesus not to send them to the Bottomless Pit. So Jesus sent them into a nearby herd of pigs. The entire herd rushed down the mountainside and into the water below, where they drowned (Luke 8:26-39). The news of Jesus' power spread quickly, and the people who lived in that town became terrified by what had happened.

Wild Boars

Wild boars are gray,

brown, or black, and have

four long, pointed teeth that

continue to grow even in adulthood.

Boars are mentioned in Psalm 80:13.

A Pig Tale

Jesus used the bad reputation of pigs to tell a beautiful story. In the parable of the Prodigal Son (Luke 15:11-32), a young man left home, wasted his money, and eventually got a job as a swineherd (a person who watches pigs). Even the thought of feeding and watching pigs was disgusting to most Jewish people. While feeding the pigs, the man realized how low he had sunk. He returned home to a loving father, who welcomed him with joy.

Domestic Pigs

Pigs are productive. One pig can produce about 150 pounds (68 kilograms) of bacon or 100 pounds (45 kilograms) of pork. Domestic pigs have 8 to 12 piglets per litter.

What happens after you wash a pig?

It goes right back to the mud and rolls in it (2 Peter 2:22).

Creepy Crawlies

The Bible mentions many kinds of creepy crawlies—snails, scorpions, spiders, worms, ants, and others. Some of these creatures, such as scorpions, were feared or hated because they were dangerous. Some, such as snails, were mainly ignored. Others, such as ants, became tools for teaching: "Take a lesson from the ants, you lazy fellow," said a wise man. "For though they have no king to make them work, yet they labor hard all summer, gathering food for the winter" (Proverbs 6:6-8).

A Snail Curse
Garden snails travel at three one-hundredths of a mile (.05 kilometers) per hour. When David wanted to curse those who were unjust, he said, "Let them be as snails that dissolve into slime" (Psalm 58:8).

Scorpions
Scorpions almost always live in hot climates and are usually two to three inches (5 to 8 centimeters) long. But some kinds can grow up to ten inches (25 centimeters) long. They attack prey with their strong pincerlike claws and pointed tail, which has a poisonous stinger that can paralyze. Scorpions usually eat insects or even mice. They won't attack humans unless they are frightened or cornered; but when they do, they deliver a very painful (but not usually fatal) sting. The book of Revelation mentions their dreaded sting (Revelation 9:1-11).

Slug

Worms
There are thousands of different kinds of worms. Some, such as tapeworms and roundworms, live as parasites inside other animals. Most worms live in water (marine worms) or under the ground (earthworms). People often regard worms with disgust. When David wanted to express how terrible he was feeling, he said, "I am a worm, not a man, scorned and despised by my own people . . ." (Psalm 22:6).

Spiders

Spiders are plentiful in Bible lands. Their webs are beautiful but fragile. One man said to Job that "a man without God is trusting in a spider's web. Everything he counts on will collapse"
(Job 8:14).

Ants: Hard Workers

The ants described in Proverbs (6:6-8 and 30:25) are most likely harvester ants. These hardworking insects

- build long tunnels in the desert near grain fields
- collect all sorts of seeds
- store the seeds away
- carry wet seeds to the surface and allow them to dry in heaps
- work without rest or aimless wandering

What kind of creepy crawly greatly upset the prophet Jonah?

A worm (Jonah 4:7).

55

Lions

The Bible mentions the lion more often than any other untamed animal. There were many lions in the lands of the Bible. They lived in the thick brush and forests along the Jordan River. Several Bible stories include lions. In one well-known story, Daniel spent a night in a den of hungry lions. The lion was often used as a symbol of power: "Judah is a young lion that has finished eating its prey. He has settled down as a lion—who will dare to rouse him?" (Genesis 49:9). As is true today, lions were considered king of the beasts (Proverbs 30:30).

Extinct

In Bible times, lions were plentiful in the Middle East. Today most wild lions live in Africa.

Lion with Cub

Lion Statues

King Solomon's throne was decorated with statues of lions. Two statues stood beside the armrests, with twelve more guarding the six steps leading up to the throne (1 Kings 10:19-20).

Lionesses

Female lions, or lionesses, do most of the hunting. The males are less effective hunters because their huge manes and roaring tend to scare off prey. Lionesses usually hunt herds rather than individual animals. They often threatened Israelite flocks of sheep and goats. When David was a shepherd, he used a club to chase off lions and defend his sheep (1 Samuel 17:34-37).

Lion Traps

Some hunters in Bible lands considered it a special challenge to capture lions alive. They would do this by digging a pit, covering it, and then baiting it. When a lion fell into the pit, they would either kill it or herd it into captivity. The Persian king Darius had a collection of captured lions, which he kept in a large park. It was this "lions' den" into which Daniel was thrown for praying to God (Daniel 6:1-24).

How did Samson kill the lion that attacked him?

He ripped its jaws apart with his bare hands (Judges 14:5-6). Note: Do not try this on your own at home!

God's Care for Animals

Grasshopper on Fern

Over and over the Bible tells about God's loving care for animals. Psalm 104 lists many ways that God takes care of them. He provides
- water for drinking
- rain to help plants grow for food
- trees for shelter
- pastures in the mountains
- day and night for sleep and activity
- the sea for sea animals to play in
    - even life itself

If animals could talk, they would have much to praise God for!

Camouflage

God created many animals with the ability to camouflage themselves. Praying mantises, for example, look so much like sticks that they are nicknamed "walking sticks." Green frogs often hide among the green vegetation growing around their watery homes. Chameleons can change colors to match their surroundings. Some animals use camouflage to hide from predators. Others use it to lie in wait for prey.

Special Treatment

In Jesus' day the people of Israel still observed the Old Testament rules about animals. Jesus himself pointed out that the Pharisees would let their animals out for water on the Sabbath (Luke 13:15) and rescue an animal that had fallen into a well (Luke 14:5). This was good, but some Pharisees treated their animals better than they treated their fellow human beings—and that disturbed Jesus very much.

From the beginning, God wanted people to treat animals well. He gave the Israelites rules about how to care for and use their animals.

Keep Control

An owner was to keep his animals under control and not let them hurt his neighbors (Exodus 21:28-30). If an animal known to be vicious hurt a person, the owner as well as the animal was punished.

No Unequal Yokes

Farmers were not to put donkeys and oxen together on the same pulling-harness (or yoke) (Deuteronomy 22:10). This was because donkeys and oxen pull with different motions. The animals could get hurt if they tried to plow together.

Take Precautions

Anyone who dug a well and didn't cover it risked paying a steep fine if his neighbor's donkey or ox fell into it (Exodus 21:33-34).

Can you match the Bible animals with the homes God created for them?

Wild Donkeys
Mountain Cliffs
Storks
Fir Trees
Wild Goats
Dens
Rock Badgers (Coneys)
Near Mountain Streams
High Mountain Pastures
Lions

Wild donkeys—near mountain streams (Psalm 104:10-11), storks—fir trees (Psalm 104:17), wild goats—high mountain pastures (Psalm 104:18), rock badgers—mountain cliffs (Psalm 104:18), lions—dens (Psalm 104:21-22).

Your Care for Animals

Today more than ever, animals need our protection. Already many animal species have become extinct (completely destroyed). Many more are in danger of becoming extinct. When the world loses an animal species, it loses part of its beauty and wonder. How we treat animals *does* matter.

God put us in charge of taking care of animals. After he created Adam and Eve, "God blessed them and told them, 'Multiply and fill the earth and subdue it; you are masters of the fish and birds and all the animals'" (Genesis 1:28). What a big responsibility!

God gave humans responsibility for the earth, and we must take care of animals and their homes (see Psalm 8:6-7). How can we do this? The Bible gives a lot of guidance.

Parrots

1. Let kindness be the rule.
The Bible reminds us to respect all of God's creation just as we respect him. Proverbs 12:10 says, "A good man is concerned for the welfare of his animals."

2. Take good care of the animals you own.
You can find some wise advice for animal care in the laws that God handed down to the Israelites through Moses. (See Exodus 21:28-36; 23:11-12; Deuteronomy 22:1-4, 10; 25:4.) These laws point out that those who own animals are responsible for them.

3. Take care of the animals' homes.
God provided each kind of animal with a home, and these homes belong to God. "The earth belongs to God! Everything in all the world is his!" (Psalm 24:1). God created each animal so that it could take advantage of its environment. For example, God made camels, coneys, mountain goats, and even grasshoppers so that they could survive in their hot, dry habitats. Knowing this, we should try to leave the natural homes of animals undisturbed. When we drive animals out of their natural homes, sometimes they cannot survive.

What do domestic animals need from their human friends?

Food, water, exercise, protection, a place to sleep, veterinary care, love . . . can you name more?

Canada Goose and Goslings

Bible Animal Challenge

Crocodile

1. What colors are the four horsemen of the apocalypse? *(Revelation 6:1-8)*

2. What animal works hard even though it has no boss? *(Proverbs 6:6-8)*

3. Which part of Egypt's livestock died in the plague of hail? *(Exodus 9:18-25)*

4. What animal can sneak into king's palaces? *(Proverbs 30:28)*

5. To which animal was the tribe of Naphtali compared? *(Genesis 49:21)*

6. How many birds did God tell Noah to take on the ark? *(Genesis 7:3)*

7. What kind of animal did God send to destroy a vine that shaded the prophet Jonah? *(Jonah 4:7)*

8. What did Benaiah kill in a pit on a snowy day? *(1 Chronicles 11:22)*

9. What animals were used as plagues on Egypt? There were four. *(Exodus 7:15–10:20)*

10. What did God create on the fifth day of creation? *(Genesis 1:20-23)*

11. When Nabal's wife, Abigail, rode out to stop David and his men from attacking her home, what kind of animal did she ride? *(1 Samuel 25:20)*

12. What do you think a "behemoth" is? *(Job 40:15-24, KJV)*

13. To what kind of animal was the tribe of Issachar compared? *(Genesis 49:14)*

14. Where was Paul when a snake bit him? *(Acts 28:3-6)*

15. Peter found a coin in what animal's mouth? *(Matthew 17:27)*

16. What was the law in Israel for an ox that harmed someone? *(Exodus 21:28-30)*

17. What kind of bird fed Elijah when he was camped by a brook? *(1 Kings 17:2-6)*

18. What kind of scavenger ate Jezebel's dead body? *(2 Kings 9:36)*

19. What kind of animal skin did John the Baptist wear? *(Matthew 3:4)*

20. What animals did Solomon buy from the Egyptians and sell to the Hittites? *(1 Kings 10:29)*

21. What miraculous animals pulled the chariot that took Elijah to heaven? *(2 Kings 2:11)*

22. What kind of animal did Abraham sacrifice instead of his son Isaac? *(Genesis 22:13)*

23. To which prowling animal was the tribe of Benjamin compared? *(Genesis 49:27)*

24. What Philistine animals pulled the Ark of the Covenant back to Israel? *(1 Samuel 6:7)*

25. What kind of animal talked back to a prophet? *(Numbers 22:28)*

26. What did Jesus serve for breakfast one morning? *(John 21:9)*

27. What amazed Agur about snakes and eagles? *(Proverbs 30:18-19)*

28. What did Jesus eat when he appeared to the disciples behind locked doors? *(Luke 24:42)*

29. What animal has a lot in common with wine? *(Proverbs 23:32)*

30. What curse did God put on the serpent in the Garden of Eden? *(Genesis 3:14-15)*

31. What animal is said to dissolve? *(Psalm 58:8)*

32. What kind of insect can ruin a bottle of perfume? *(Ecclesiastes 10:1)*

33. Is the lion a symbol for good or evil? *(Revelation 5:5; 13:2)*

34. What part of the elephant did Solomon import for his throne? *(1 Kings 10:18)*

35. What do you think a "leviathan" is? *(Job 41:1-34)*

Mountain Sheep

36. What kind of animals ran off a cliff and drowned? *(Matthew 8:32)*

37. Moses' rod turned into what kind of animal? *(Exodus 4:3)*

38. What two birds did Noah send out of the ark to look for dry land? *(Genesis 8:6-12)*

39. What did King Rehoboam say he would use on the people of Israel? *(1 Kings 12:11)*

40. What kind of animal may bite someone who tears down an old wall? *(Ecclesiastes 10:8-9)*

41. To what animal did Jesus compare some of the Pharisees? *(Matthew 23:33)*

42. What was the only animal to lie? *(Genesis 3:4)*

43. What kind of animals did the locusts in John's vision look like? *(Revelation 9:7)*

44. Isaiah predicted a time when children could play safely with what kind of dangerous animal? *(Isaiah 11:8)*

45. To which sneaky animal was the tribe of Dan compared? *(Genesis 49:17)*

46. What predator will goats no longer fear in heaven? *(Isaiah 11:6)*

47. To what two kinds of animals did David compare himself when Saul chased him? *(1 Samuel 24:14)*

48. What kind of animal caused Herod's death? *(Acts 12:23)*

49. What destructive insect may eat our earthly treasures? *(Luke 12:33)*

50. John the Baptist ate a steady diet of what kind of animal? *(Mark 1:6)*

51. When the spies came back from spying out the Promised Land and told about the giants, they said they felt as small as what kind of animal? *(Numbers 13:33)*

52. What kind of insects did the Pharisees strain out of their drinking water? *(Matthew 23:24)*

53. What animal's home is compared to the wicked person's hope? *(Job 8:14-15)*

54. David compared his best friend to what two animals? *(2 Samuel 1:23)*

Mandrill

55. What animal did Peter say Satan is like? *(1 Peter 5:8)*

56. What kind of animals did Abel take care of? *(Genesis 4:2)*

57. When we sin, what animals are we like? *(Isaiah 53:6)*

58. When God judges us, he will separate the righteous from the unrighteous, just as a shepherd separates what two animals? *(Matthew 25:32)*

59. In the Parable of the Lost Sheep, how many sheep were in the field? *(Matthew 18:12)*

60. Amos tells of a shepherd who tried to rescue a sheep from a lion. Which animal parts were snatched from the lion's mouth? *(Amos 3:12)*

61. Nathan told David a story about a man who had only one pet. What kind of animal was it? *(2 Samuel 12:1-3)*

62. What four animals did Daniel dream about? *(Daniel 7:1-7)*

63. When the Israelites conquered Jericho, the priests blew trumpets made from the horns of what kind of animal? *(Joshua 6:4)*

64. What two kinds of animals was Saul going to sacrifice in disobedience to God? *(1 Samuel 15:15)*

65. When God carried the Israelites out of Egypt, he was said to be acting like what animal? *(Deuteronomy 32:11*

66. What animal is named for where it hides? *(Proverbs 30:26)*

67. What kinds of animals did the king of Moab use to pay Israel an annual tribute? *(2 Kings 3:4)*

68. Which king in the Bible had a great interest in mammals, birds, snakes, and fish? *(1 Kings 4:33)*

69. Zechariah had a vision of two women flying towards him with wings like what kind of birds? *(Zechariah 5:9)*

70. What animal made Peter cry? *(Luke 22:60-62)*

71. What was so unusual about the animals that Peter saw in his vision? *(Acts 10:12)*

72. What kind of animal represents the Holy Spirit? *(Mark 1:10)*

73. What kind of animals were told by an angel to eat the bodies of people who died in battle? *(Revelation 19:17-18)*

74. The prophet Micah said he would wail like what kind of animal? *(Micah 1:8)*

75. What animals did Solomon import? *(2 Chronicles 9:21, 24)*

76. What kind of animals did Elijah predict would eat Ahab's family? *(1 Kings 21:24)*

77. With what animals did Job compare himself to show how friendless he was? *(Job 30:28-29)*

78. The person who waits upon the Lord is like what animal? *(Isaiah 40:31)*

79. The person who gets rich unjustly is like what animal? *(Jeremiah 17:11)*

Animal Finder

An index of animals you can find in the Bible

A

Ant   Proverbs 6:6-7; 30:25

Antelope. *See* Deer

Ape   1 Kings 10:22; 2 Chronicles 9:21

B

Bat   Leviticus 11:19

Bear   1 Samuel 17:34-37; 2 Samuel 17:8; 2 Kings 2:23-24; Proverbs 28:15; Hosea 13:8; Revelation 13:2

Bee   Judges 14:8; Isaiah 7:18

Behemoth   Job 40:15-24, KJV

Bird   Genesis 8:7; Exodus 16:13; Leviticus 11:13-19; Deuteronomy 14:12-17; 1 Samuel 26:20; 1 Kings 17:1-6; 2 Chronicles 9:21; Isaiah 34:11; Jeremiah 17:11; Hosea 11:11; Zechariah 2:14; Revelation 18:2

Bull (male cattle)   Leviticus 4:3; 1 Kings 7:25; Hebrews 10:4

C

Camel   Genesis 24:61-64; Leviticus 11:4; 1 Samuel 15:3; Ezra 2:66; Zechariah 14:15; Matthew 3:4; 23:24; Luke 18:25

Cat. *See* Leopard, Lion

Cattle. *See* Ox

Chameleon. *See* Lizard

Chicken. *See* Fowl

Cormorant   Leviticus 11:17

Cow, Cattle. *See* Ox

D

Deer (antelope, doe, gazelle, hart, roe deer, roe buck)   Genesis 25:27; Deuteronomy 14:4-5; 2 Samuel 2:18; 1 Kings 4:23; Psalm 42:1; Song of Solomon 8:14; Isaiah 35:6

Dog   Exodus 11:7; Judges 7:5; 1 Samuel 17:43; Psalm 59:6; Proverbs 26:11; Ecclesiastes 9:4; 2 Peter 2:22; Revelation 22:15

Donkey   Genesis 22:3; Exodus 20:17; Numbers 22:21-31; Deuteronomy 5:14; Joshua 15:18; Judges 15:14-17; Ezra 2:66; Proverbs 26:3; Zechariah 9:9; Matthew 21:7

Dove (pigeon)   Genesis 8:8; 15:9; Leviticus 12:8; Isaiah 38:14; Matthew 3:16; 10:16; Luke 2:24

Dragon   Deuteronomy 32:33; Psalm 91:13; 148:7; Isaiah 27:1; 51:9; Job 30:29; Malachi 1:3; Ezekiel 29:3; Micah 1:8; Revelation 12:3; 13:2; 16:13; 20:2

E

Eagle   Deuteronomy 28:49; 32:11-12; Psalm 103:5; Proverbs 30:19; Jeremiah 48:40; 49:16; Ezekiel 17:3, 7

Earthworm. *See* Worm

Ewe (female sheep)   Leviticus 22:28; 2 Samuel 12:3

F

Fish   Deuteronomy 4:18; Nehemiah 13:16; Psalm 8:8; Jonah 2:10; Matthew 4:19; 17:27; Luke 11:11; 24:42; John 21:10

Flea   1 Samuel 24:14; 26:20

Fly   Exodus 8:20-32; Isaiah 7:18

Fowl (chicken, hen, rooster)   1 Kings 4:23; Matthew 23:37; 26:34; Mark 14:30

Fox   Nehemiah 4:3; Luke 13:32

Frog   Exodus 8:2-13; Psalm 105:30; Revelation 16:13

G

Gazelle. *See* Deer

Gnat   Matthew 23:24

Goat (wild goat, ibex)   Exodus 23:19; Leviticus 3:12; 9:15; 16:1-34; Numbers 29; Deuteronomy 14:4-5; Proverbs 30:31

Goose. *See* Fowl

Grasshopper. *See* Locust

H

Hare   Leviticus 11:6; Deuteronomy 14:7

Hawk   Deuteronomy 14:15; Job 39:26

Heron   Leviticus 11:19; Deuteronomy 14:18

Hog (wild boar). *See* Pig

Hoopoe (lapwing)   Leviticus 11:19

Hornet   Exodus 23:28

Horse   Genesis 47:17; Exodus 14:9; 15:1, 19, 21; Deuteronomy 17:16; Joshua 11:4-9; Ezra 2:66; Esther 8:10, 14; Psalm 20:7; 33:17; 147:10; Jeremiah 5:8; 8:16; 47:3; 50:11; Habakkuk 1:8; Revelation 6:1-8; 19:11-16.

Hyena   Jeremiah 50:39

JK

Jackal   Lamentations 4:3

Kid (young goat)   Genesis 37:31; Exodus 23:19; Judges 6:19; Luke 15:29

Kite. *See* Hawk

L

Lamb (young sheep)   Genesis 22:8; Exodus 12:21; 2 Samuel 12:4; Isaiah 11:6; 53:7; Mark 14:12; John 1:29; Acts 8:32; 1 Corinthians 5:7; 1 Peter 1:19; Revelation 5:6; 17:14

Leech   Proverbs 30:15

Leopard   Isaiah 11:6; Jeremiah 5:6; 13:23; Daniel 7:6; Hosea 13:7; Habakkuk 1:8; Revelation 13:2

Leviathan   Job 41:1-34(KJV); Psalm 74:14(KJV); 104:26(KJV); Isaiah 27:1

Lice (gnat)   Exodus 8:16-19

Lion   Judges 14:5-8; 1 Samuel 17:34-37; Jeremiah 5:6; Ezekiel 19:1-9; 1 Peter 5:8; Revelation 5:5; 13:2

Lizard   Leviticus 11:29-30; Proverbs 30:28

Locust (grasshopper)   Exodus 10:4-19; Leviticus 11:22-23; John 3:4

M

Monkey. *See* Ape

Moth   Job 27:18; Isaiah 59:5; Hosea 5:12; Matthew 6:19; Luke 12:33

Mouse. *See* Rat

Mule   Leviticus 19:19; 2 Samuel 18:9; Ezra 2:66

OP

Ostrich   Job 39:13-18

Owl   Leviticus 11:16-18; Psalm 102:6; Isaiah 34:11-15; Jeremiah 50:39

Ox (adult bull)   Exodus 21:28-29; Deuteronomy 14:4-5; Nehemiah 5:18; Psalm 106:20; Proverbs 14:4; Isaiah 11:7; Luke 14:5; 1 Timothy 5:18

Pig (swine)   Leviticus 11:7; Deuteronomy 14:8; Isaiah 66:17; Matthew 7:6; 8:30-32; Luke 15:15-16; 2 Peter 2:22

Pigeon. *See* Dove

QR

Quail   Exodus 16:13; Numbers 11:31; Psalm 105:40

Rabbit. *See* Hare

Ram (male sheep)   Genesis 22:13; Daniel 8:3

Rat   Leviticus 11:29; Isaiah 6:4-13

Raven   Genesis 8:7; Leviticus 11:15; 1 Kings 17:1-7

Rock Badger (coney)   Leviticus 11:5; Psalm 104:18; Proverbs 30:26

S

Scorpion   Deuteronomy 8:15; Ezekiel 2:6; Luke 11:11-12; Revelation 9:5

Serpent. *See* Snake

Sheep   1 Samuel 17:34-35; Psalm 23:1-6; Luke 15:1-7; John 10:1-12; Revelation 5:6-13

Snail   Psalm 58:8

Snake (adder, asp, cobra, viper)   Genesis 3:1-24; Numbers 21:4-9; 2 Kings 18:1-4; Proverbs 30:19; Isaiah 11:8-9; 59:5; Amos 5:19; Matthew 7:10; John 3:14-15; Acts 28:1-6

Sparrow   Psalm 84:3; Matthew 10:29

Spider   Job 8:14-15; Isaiah 59:5-6

Stork   Leviticus 11:19; Jeremiah 8:7

Swine. *See* Pig

TVW

Turtledove. *See* Dove

Vulture   Leviticus 11:13; Matthew 24:28

Wasp. *See* Hornet

Wolf   Isaiah 11:6; 65:25; Habakkuk 1:8; Matthew 7:15; Luke 10:3; John 10:12; Acts 20:29

Worm (earthworm)   Job 17:14; Psalm 22:6; Isaiah 41:14; 66:24